HAVE A PRODUCT IDEA?

HOW MANY COULD YOU SELL?

Leonie Mateer

Published in the United States of America

ISBN-13 978-0-9976574-9-4

1.Non-Fiction/ Business/ Marketing
2. Non Fiction / Self Help/ Business / Marketing/New Business

1.5.17

CONTENTS

CHAPTER 1

I HAVE A PRODUCT IDEA – WHAT DO I DO?

Almost everyone has a great idea at some time in his or her life. It could be a new baby carrier or a new type of gadget.

Often people would tell me that they had an idea and a couple of years later they would see their idea sitting on a store shelf. "I thought of that!" they would say. "I could have done that".

Yes, they are right. They could have done that. The difference, however, is I DID it. And you can do it too! For many years I have taken an idea of a product and taken it all the way to sitting on 30,000 store shelves.

The type of products I have created, marketed and sold fall into many product categories: toys, games, calendars, clocks, teen cosmetics, cosmetic organizers, bath products and more...

It doesn't matter what product you are about to launch into the marketplace – the basic journey is the same.

So how do you take a product idea to market?

When I had the my first real big product idea– it took only six months to get my idea from just an idea in my mind to an actual product sitting on hundreds of store shelves. It only took eighteen months to get the products onto thirty thousand store shelves. It took three short years to make the product a profitable branded product line - a brand that could house a number of different product categories and a brand that would become substantially more valuable than the original product.

Where should you start?

Visualization – If you can visualize it – your can make it

Focus Groups – Focus groups give your product credibility and provide much needed product, brand and category information

Documenting your Vision – Taking your idea from mind to paper to prototype to finished product

Researching your product category and the industry

Creating & developing your product and your brand

Defining your consumer market – Who is your consumer? Are you sure?

Researching the size of your consumer market – The size of your market determines your potential sales

Licensing or Manufacturing your idea – What choices do you have?

Setting up your rep force – Your reps are your gateway to your retail buyers

Marketing & Selling your product – Trade & Consumer Shows, Sales Collateral needs

Establishing yourself in the Marketplace

It sounds daunting – but with an easy step-by-step approach you will be amazed how easy it is to get your product idea to market.

Please check out each chapter dedicated to specific topics from focus groups, manufacturing to setting up your first trade show and hiring your sales reps and much more.

CHAPTER 2

PROPEL YOUR PRODUCT IDEA INTO THE MARKETPLACE

How do you do it? Take a product idea or an invention and turn it into a business?

1. Take your idea and turn it into a **visual image** immediately.

2. Paste it somewhere where you can see it often throughout the day. Its repetitive image, before long, becomes your springboard to making it a reality.

3. Make your "new idea" the first image you see when you wake in the morning and the last image you see when you go to sleep at night.

It is a simple trick but it works!!

Visualization is the key to your success.

Taking your product idea and propelling it forward into the future needs constant nurturing.

A neglected vision simply dissipates if your attention is removed from it.

Take your idea and create an image that best depicts your idea's personality, features, design, colors, shape etc. – Your first image can be simple and undeveloped.

One of the Main rules of marketing:
Keep all your logos, visuals, themes, and messages the **SAME** in all advertising, packaging, promotions and materials.

It takes many, many times for consumers to identify with you... so keeping the message and the visuals constant creates consumer awareness for you, your business and your products.

If your idea is starting a new business... create a visual of what your new business represents – It could be a simple mock-up of your home page of your new website, or simply a brand logo idea with your product idea.

Once you have your visual – it is time to ask yourself some important questions:

• **What type** of business do you want to be?

• Will you want to **expand** your new business into other areas or services?

• **How big** do you want your business to be? i.e. owner operated with no staff? Hiring independent contractors or staff when needed? Etc.

• Do you want your business to be **local** or expand **internationally**?

• Do you want to **partner** up with local complimentary type businesses to promote your products/services along with them?
• **How many hours** per day do you want to work? What percentage of these hours do you want to dedicate to building your business, maintaining your business and promoting your business?

• What areas do you **need assistance** in developing your idea/product/service? I.e. product development, packaging, manufacturing, promotion, advertising, marketing, sales, social networking etc....

• What are your **strengths? Weaknesses**? Note your weaknesses are usually jobs YOU DONT LIKE TO DO!!

• Who are your competitors? How many are there?

• What sets your business apart from other similar businesses? What is your niche?

• **How big is the market** you are going to be entering? What size is the industry/category? Etc.

• Have you done your **sales projections** based on your ideal working situation?

• Can you make this business a **financial success** if you can generate the projected sales?

It is also imperative that you know where your idea's final resting place will be...for example; your own website, store shelves, on-line retailer sites.

If your idea is a new book – create a visual of your front cover (it will change, of course, when your publisher or graphic designer takes over) and go into a bookstore and imagine your new book sitting on the shelf.

Visualize your book in all its product categories: i.e. paperback, eBook, and audio book...   Is your book the first of a collection of books? What do they all look like sitting on a shelf?

If your idea is a new product, visit a store and imagine your product sitting on the shelf.   Add this to your visual.

As your "idea" begins to take form – keep updating your visual. Before long your visual will have become a reality.

CHAPTER 3

30 TIPS ON TAKING YOUR PRODUCT IDEA TO MARKET

1. Create a Visual of your Idea. – Visualize your product at its final resting place – on a store shelf – or in your   consumer's hands.

2. Create a name for your product

3. Set up your product development work area – computers/printers/cameras etc.

4. Create a description of your product

5. Create product profile

6. Expand your product into 3 separate products – price and/or color, style etc.

7. Visit a store that carries your type of product and look at colors, prices, sizes etc.

8. Create an image of your product with Photoshop

9. Create a product name design, brand name and logo

10. Create your packaging

11. Protect yourself legally with copyrights and patents

12. Download all the necessary legal documents i.e. confidentiality agreements etc.

13. Research your product category

14. Find out the size of the industry

15. Research who your consumer is

16. How big is your consumer market

17. Focus your product in focus groups with your potential consumers

18. Keep all your focus group information and industry information on file

19. Research your customers (buyers) who are they? – How many are there?

20. Research companies who may license your product idea

21. Research custom domestic and international
        manufacturers who are experienced in your type
of   product

22. Research warehousing, shipping & distribution
options

23. Research trade shows relevant to your product's
industry

24. Have sample products developed for sales
brochures & initial presentations

25. Hire independent reps to sell your product into the
marketplace

26. Prepare your sales materials

27. Research all your product, marketing and
distribution costs

28. Create your price sheets – Retailers, Distributors,
International etc.

29. Develop a marketing program – consumer & trade
advertising, social media, PR.

30. Set up your company.

CHAPTER 4

SETTING UP A NEW BUSINESS

What you need to ask yourself!

• What TYPE of business do you want it to be?

• Will you want to EXPAND your business into other categories or services?

• What will you NAME your product/service? Your product/service is separate from your BRAND name.

• Will your business be: LOCAL • NATIONAL• GLOBAL?

• Will you want to PARTNER UP with complimentary businesses to promote your products or services?

• How many HOURS do you want to dedicate to your new business? i.e. Building your business, maintaining your business and promoting your business.

• What areas do you need ASSISTANCE for developing your idea/product/service?
> Product design and development?
> Packaging – Point of Purchase
> Packaging/promotion?
> Manufacturing?
> Warehousing
> Marketing
> Sales
> Promotion
> Social Media
> Finance

• What are YOUR STRENGTHS and WEAKNESSES? Your weaknesses are usually what you don't like to do.

• Who are your COMPETITORS? How many are there?

• What sets your business APART from other similar businesses? What is your niche?

• How BIG is the MARKET you are entering? What size is the industry?

• Who is going to be your CONSUMER? What age? What sex? What characteristics?

• Have you run consumer FOCUS GROUPS? Did your idea get 85% approval?

• Have you done your SALES PROJECTIONS based on your ideal working situation?

• What will be your COSTS? Have you researched all your potential expenses?

• Can you make your business a FINANCIAL SUCCESS based on your sales projections and expenses?

• It is imperative that you VISUALIZE your product/service success. Where is its final resting place? Stores shelves? Satisfied user?

CHAPTER 5

TIPS FOR PROTECTING YOUR PRODUCT IDEA.

I often get asked, "what if my product idea gets stolen?" or "if I show my product idea to a licensor or a manufacturer what prevents them from just knocking off my idea?

This fear often has crippled a product inventor's progress to such an extent that they are still fearfully holding onto their idea and instead of their product sitting on the shelf – they are still sitting on the fence and their idea has been frozen in time.

I do, however, agree that it pays to be cautious when exposing your product concept to others. Today you can simply download Confidentiality Agreements, Non Disclosure agreements and

Independent Contractor Agreements – saving a small fortune in legal fees.

I recommend that product inventors have everyone who is exposed to initial product concepts and designs sign an appropriate document in order to protect themselves. This includes: graphic artists, product designers, manufacturers, rep, temps, employees etc.

However, you can never protect yourself 100%.

So once you have executed the appropriate legal documents to protect yourself it is time to move on and accept the fact that it is the first one to market who takes the prize.

Most serious investors will not sign a confidentiality agreement. Which is a problem. They do not want to limit their options by eliminating a whole class of ventures. However, lawyers and attorneys usually insist on an investor signing a confidentiality agreement in an attempt to protect your "idea or product." You can see this is a grey area. Always get the best legal advice. It can be a difficult choice to make. Again, it is the first to market at the best price that is your protection.

And there is another problem - you can't "own" an idea.

Patents protect inventions, copyright protects creative works, and trademarks protect commercial words and images. Nothing legally protects an idea. You don't own it.

The only way you really protect an idea is to build a company, launch it, bring it to market and stake out your territory like an explorer planting a flag. You'll want to be so good and so fast that no larger company copies it and beats you at your own game. Copying is excruciatingly legal in our economy.

Imitation is the biggest form of flattery!   Ouch

You just have to be the first one out there – with a quality product and at the best price.

Your Brand is what will give your idea its value.

So being the first Brand to market enables you to create consumer awareness and this, in turn, establishes your credibility in the marketplace and solidifies your position as number one.

So make sure that you trademark your product name (if unique) and your brand name and copyright your designs.

CHAPTER 6

WHO IS YOUR CONSUMER?

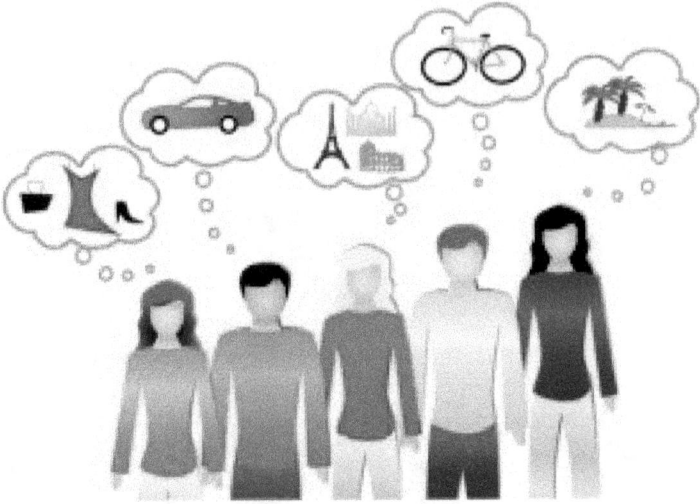

Is your consumer really who you think they are?

When you have a new product or a new idea that you want to launch – the question is – **"to whom?"**

Who is going to be your new consumer?

If your consumer is a baby – it's simple – your consumer market to whom you will be advertising and promoting your product to is pregnant women, new   mothers, new   parents   and new grandparents

If your consumer is a toddler – it is the parents and grandparents again.

If your consumer is a preteen – your consumer market is both the pre teen and the parent

If your consumer is a teen – your consumer market is the teen not the parent – no teen will buy what their parents want to buy.

And so on.

However, beware, your consumer market can change...

What is hot with teens today – is hot with preteens tomorrow and can even stray down to the kiddie market and then your teen brand is destroyed!

It is very easy to lose your consumer base if you are not constantly researching and **focusing your consumer.**

Your consumer base affects your Brand image and its value!

If you are a teen brand and you lose the support of your core consumer your Brand can lose credibility in the marketplace.

Constantly go back to your what your Brand represents.

Keep a loyal image for your consumers

If you want to develop an idea, a product and a new brand – then thoroughly research who your new consumer is.

Ensure that your marketing efforts are targeting your core consumer at all times.

Don't try to be everything to everybody! Do your research! Keep focused!

CHAPTER 7

TIPS FOR RUNNING A CONSUMER FOCUS GROUP

Listen to your focus groups – their input is worth gold

I was doing consumer focus groups before focus groups became a necessary tool in the product development and marketing process.

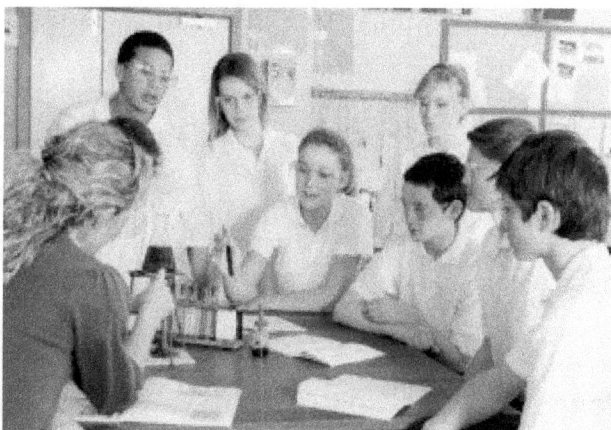

Focus groups, focus groups, and focus groups!!

I cannot emphasize enough how important it is to

involve your consumer in every stage of your product development, brand development and marketing programs.

We ran focus groups in a local San Diego high school on a bi-monthly basis for many, many years. One hundred teen girls per session and three sessions a day gave us immediate input.

Involving our consumer with our product development gave us the EDGE over our competitors.

We knew what was hot today, not yesterday. Teens kept us ahead of the trends... they were making the trends... and, before long, we became the teen trend experts.

We were constantly keeping retailer buyers and trade editors informed of what our focus groups were telling us.

• Follow every question with a "WHY?" You learn more from the 'WHY'S"

• Make every questionnaire (one per group) no more than two pages

Name, Address, Gender, Contact should be asked at all times.

• Don't be a salesperson. Leave your EGO at home. You are there to learn not to sell. Your product has to SELL ITSELF in 4 ½ seconds on a store shelf.

• Have every participant sign a TALENT RELEASE form. This allows their photos and comments to be used on sales and promotional materials. Consumer photos and endorsements are valuable sales and marketing vehicles.

• Focus group participants should qualify as your END consumer. Choose a minimum of 10-15 participants for each group. A total of 1500 participants give the most accurate read. Even 50-100 helps towards product credibility

• Do not use the SAME participants for each focus group. One participant can influence the whole group. If focusing DIFFERENT products or concepts you can use the same group.

• If you are not getting the RESULTS you want. Is it the RIGHT consumer? Is it the PRODUCT at fault? Best to find out NOW so you can make the necessary changes.

• Ask the SAME questions. Repeat the most important questions so you get an accurate read over multiple focus groups. Add more questions as you develop your product, packaging and brand image.

• If you don't get 85% acceptance – go back to the drawing board.

CHAPTER 8

10 TIPS FOR CREATING A BRAND

1. Your Brand's LIFE IS LIMITLESS

A Brand is not just an image, a logo and a slogan – it is a PERSONALITY

YOUR BRAND is a LIVING BREATHING ENTITY of what your idea represents

Your BRAND is your most VALUABLE ASSET

2. NAME YOUR BRAND

Choose a name that will work as an UMBRELLA for many different product categories – don't limit your future growth.

Choose a name that has both visual and verbal global appeal

Your BRAND NAME should have instant appeal and be whole-heartedly embraced by your targeted consumer

3. Your **BRAND** name should match your **DOMAIN NAME**

4. WHAT IS YOUR BRAND?

If your BRAND were an animal – what animal would it be?

If your BRAND were a plant – what plant would it be?

If your BRAND were a famous person – who would it be?

5. WHAT IS YOUR BRAND'S PERSONALITY?

Remove advertisements from consumer magazines that feature your type of consumer or products.

Observe the typeface, logos, colors, and style of

these ads and the people featured in the ads.

Write down a list of 20 adjectives that best describes your type of consumer. I.e. male, strong, browns, or female, soft, pink or kinds, yellow, energetic, happy.

6. HOW FAR WILL YOUR BRAND STRETCH?

Create a list of what product categories you could create under your BRAND umbrella

Once your BRAND has matured and earned value – you can license your brand to other companies to create, market and sell products that fall into different, but complimentary product categories.

Remember that all these product categories will be marketed to your existing targeted consumer.

7. WHAT IS YOUR BRAND STATEMENT?

Create one sentence that best describes your Brand.

Start by writing all the adjectives that best describe your BRAND – not your product.

Keep your statement very general to allow for company and brand growth.

8. CREATE YOUR LOGO

Choose a number of logos from various websites, magazines and searches that are similar in style and design to what you want to achieve. Do an image search online.

Incorporate your collected adjectives into your creative process.

Choose a logo that best depicts your Brand image and promise

9. DO A LEGAL SEARCH

Do a brand name/domain name search to check availability

Always have 2 or 3 back up names in case your first choice is not available.

Decide in which product categories/industries you want to copyright your brand.

It is more cost effective to copyright your BRAND name along with your "MARK" (logo)

10. YOUR BRAND IS YOUR BIGGEST ASSET

A consumer product's life is LIMITED
A product line allows innovation and growth
A BRAND 's life is LIMITLESS

Your product idea is a seed
Your product line is a row of plants
Your BRAND is the NURSERY

You are the watering can

CHAPTER 9

HAVE A PRODUCT IDEA? HOW MANY COULD YOU SELL?

Lets have some fun and work out how many products you could sell to the USA retail market

(1) Use the list of USA Retailers (pages 38-41) to project your potential annual sales for the USA

First, locate the **type of stores** that would carry your product idea.

Then add the **total number of stores** that could carry your item.

A. Total number of Stores: _____

(b) Next work out what the total number of products you could sell per store? ___

I.e. Calculate how many turns (re-orders per year) per store. (E.g. 3 or 4 for general merchandise)

(C) This gives you a potential number of products (units) you could sell per year to retailers in the USA.

Sample: USA
A. Number of Stores:		**30,000**
Products per store	12	
Turns per year (4)	**x 4**	
B. Total products ps.	48	**x 48**

C.   Total products per year   1,440,000

Of course some stores will not turn your products four times a year…. Turns can vary. Deep discounters turn products more often.

(2) Now work out how big your **consumer base is.**

Research the **NUMBER of Consumers** who may purchase **your type of product idea** i.e.

Number of teens in the USA = 25.6 million (Teen product idea)

Number of births in the USA – 6 million (baby product)

Number of people who fish in the USA - 45.7 million (fishing product)

(3) Use your consumer FOCUS GROUPS to calculate what percentage of your consumers would purchase your type of product idea

I.e. 6 million baby products sold. 80% of consumers say YES to purchase your baby product.. you have a potential consumer base of 4.8 million consumers

You can only sell as many products as your consumer base allows.

TOP 100 STORES IN THE USA (2016)

Rank	Company	#Stores
1	Wal-Mart Stores	5,109
2	The Kroger Co.	3,730
3	Costco	464
4	The Home Depot	1,965
5	Walgreen	8,157
6	Target	1,790
7	CVS Caremark	7,808
8	Lowe's Companies	1,793

9	Amazon.com	N/A
10	Safeway	1,326
11	Best Buy	1,445
12	McDonald's	14,350
13	Publix Super Markets	1,296
14	Apple Store / iTunes	259
15	Macy's	821
16	Rite Aid	4,570
17	Royal Ahold / Ahold USA	768
18	Sears Holdings	1,659
19	TJX	2,569
20	H-E-B Grocery	317
21	YUM! Brands	17,326
22	Albertsons	1,108
23	Kohl's	1,162
24	Dollar General	11,789
25	Delhaize America	1,361
26	Meijer	213
27	WakeFern / ShopRite	330
28	Ace Hardware	4,251
29	BJ's Wholesale Club	210
30	Whole Foods Market	381
31	Doctor's Assoc. / Subway	27,062
32	Nordstrom	283
33	Gap	2,465
34	AT&T Wireless	2,156
35	J.C. Penney Co.	1,063
36	Aldi	1,376
37	Bed Bath & Beyond	1,466
38	SUPERVALU	1,557
39	7-Eleven	8,154
40	Ross Stores	1,361
41	Verizon Wireless	7,024

42	Starbucks	12,560
43	Family Dollar Stores	8,042
44	Bi-Lo	800
45	L Brands	2,685
46	Menard	287
47	Trader Joe's	447
48	Wendy's	5,750
49	Burger King Worldwide	7,128
50	Dollar Tree	5,157
51	Hy-Vee	236
52	Army / Air Force Exchange	610
53	Dunkin' Brands Group	10,566
54	Health Mart Systems	3,419
55	AutoZone	4,947
56	Toys "R" Us	1,132
57	Wegmans Food Market	85
58	O'Reilly Automotive	4,366
59	DineEquity	3,449
60	Giant Eagle	429
61	Sherwin-Williams	3,764
62	Dick's Sporting Goods	695
63	Staples	1,364
64	Office Depot	1,745
65	Dillard's	297
66	Good Neighbor Pharmacy	3,096
67	Darden Restaurants	2,174
68	GameStop	4,198
69	PetSmart	1,291
70	QVC	N/A
71	Chick-fil-A	1,890
72	WinCo Foods	98
73	Tractor Supply Co.	1,382
74	Barnes & Noble	1,364

75	A&P	283
76	AVB Brandsource	3,018
77	Signet Jewelers	2,868
78	Foot Locker	2,369
79	Big Lots	1,460
80	Hudson's Bay	165
81	Alimentation Couche-Tard	4,044
82	Defense Commissary Agency	179
83	Neiman Marcus	87
84	Jack in the Box	2,888
85	Ascena Retail Group	3,834
86	Burlington Coat Factory	530
87	Ikea North America Services	40
88	Williams-Sonoma	594
89	Save Mart Supermarkets	217
90	Panera Bread Company	1,880
91	Advance Auto Parts	4,098
92	Michaels Stores	1,170
93	True Value Co.	4,602
94	Domino's Pizza	5,067
95	Belk	297
96	Chipotle Mexican Grill	1,766
97	Sonic	3,518
98	Stater Bros. Holdings	167
99	Price Chopper Supermarkets	135
100	Dell	N/A
		293023

Research retailers from the countries you wish to export your product to and do the same calculations to establish your potential worldwide sales.

Note these are brick and mortar stores - you will
need to calculate online retailer potential sales also.

CHAPTER 10

WAL-MART TARGET K MART – GET YOUR PRODUCT IDEA OR INVENTION ONTO RETAIL SHELVES!

"As you walk down the isle of a mass retail store and look at the thousands of products on the shelves you can rest assured that every one of those products started with a vision.

When I first decided to take my product idea to retail. I had no idea where to start or what to do.

thirty years later and many products, brands and companies later, I discovered that I had found– a simple step-by-step formula for taking a product idea to retail.

Here are some basic steps –

It all begins with being able to **visualize** your product sitting on the shelves of 30,000 retail stores...

(If you don't know where you are going – nowhere is where you will end up)

Expand your product idea into multiple colors/sizes/styles to create a product line. The best selling item is often a hybrid of the original concept (See Chapter 12)

Create a product name and brand name (A product's life is limited – a brand is limitless)

A product line gives credibility – A Brand is your biggest asset)

Put your idea on paper – Choose the right tools to capture the vision.

Run **focus groups** to obtain consumer input and credibility

Define your consumer market – **Who is your consumer?** Are you sure?

Create your packaging – What are your **packaging options** for retail?

Develop your product **samples & prototypes**

License or Manufacture? Sourcing your options

Hiring your reps – What you can expect from your retail rep.

Researching your retail category and industry – Become an expert in your product's retail world

Your POP (point of purchase) display options

Everyday (planogram) vs. Promotional

Marketing and Promotions – Consumer & Trade

Manufacturing, Distribution, Shipping

Going on the Road Show – Sales materials

Trade Shows

Pricing your product – cost and retail

Pricing your product is key to its success. If you are the first to market with your product idea and it is unique and different from other products on the market your entry price point will establish the product's conceived value for the future. Choosing a retail price that is too low or pricing your product too high are just as bad as each other.

Your price, of course, has to include your raw manufacturing costs, shipping costs, warehousing costs, retail promotional costs, rep commissions, branding/advertising costs and in order to reach a reasonable retail price you have to include your retailers margin which can range from 10-15% for deep discounters to 50% for many mass retailers.

I.e. your sheet price is $5.00.. it retails for $10.00 (50% margin)

Always check the retail prices of competitive products on the retail shelves. If you cannot compete with them.. you have to go back to the drawing board.

CHAPTER 11

"SELL- IN" DOESN'T MEAN, "SELL - THROUGH"

"

What is "Sell in"?

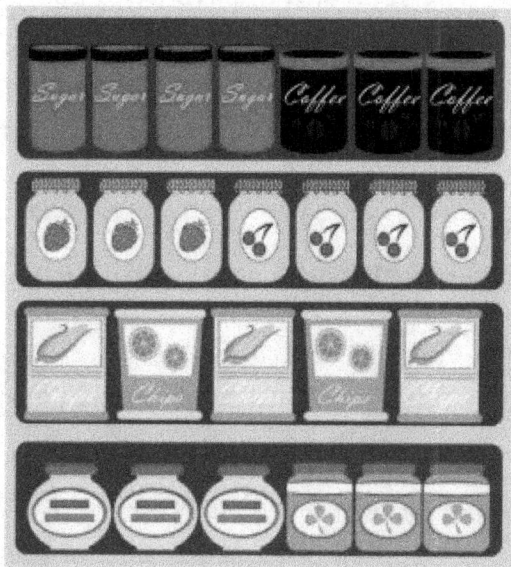

"SELL IN" IS WHEN YOU THINK YOU HAVE FINALLY MADE IT.

You have done all the hard work... taken your product idea from a simple concept in your mind through every stage of development – and you have finally sold your product/s to Wal-Mart, Target, K Mart and many more major retail stores.

YOUR PRODUCT IS ON THEIR SHELVES – LOOKING GOOD. THAT IS "SELL IN"

But, wait.... You are not even half way there....

"SELL THROUGH" IS WHAT IT IS ALL ABOUT...
FINANCIAL SUCCESS and BRAND SUCCESS - THAT IS.

You don't make a cent until a consumer has purchased your product – That is "sell through".

"Sell Through" determines if your product idea is a success or a failure.

So how do you prevent a disaster waiting for you once your product is sitting pretty on a retail shelf?

Focus groups, focus groups, focus groups.

If you don't get an 85% acceptance rate from your focus groups - you can't expect the desired "sell through" once your product hits the store shelves.

No amount of advertising can convince a consumer to buy your product if the desire and need factors are not met.

It is imperative to get consumer feed back during ALL stages of your product's development process.

CHAPTER 12

EXPANDING YOUR PRODUCT IDEA INTO A PRODUCT LINE

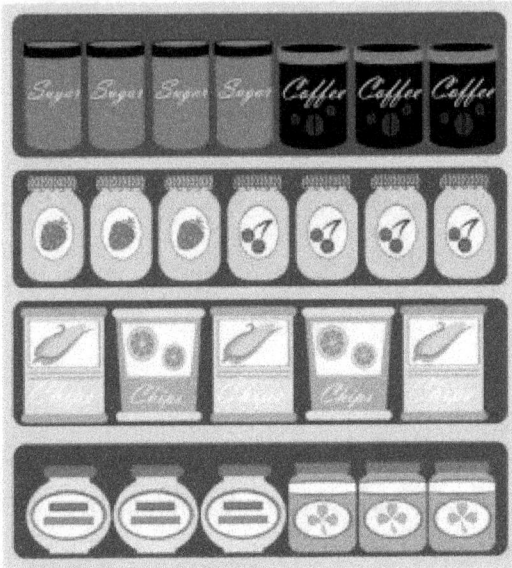

In order to capture shelf space in a retail store it is much more attractive to the buyer, and much more credible to the industry, if you take your product idea (concept) and expand it into a product line.

A single product usually has a lifespan of eighteen months – Ouch

A product line gives your idea **staying power**

Very seldom do you make money from a single item

Often the best selling item is a **hybrid of your original concept**

A product line is more credible to the industry

Capture more real estate at retail with a line of products

Take your original idea and multiply it by three

Expand your product concept/uniqueness into multiple products: Color • Style • **Price**

Visualize and document your line of products on a three-foot retail shelf.

If your product idea is unique you may be creating a new category!

A product line gives your consumer a choice and gives your retail buyer a viable new line to introduce at store level

CHAPTER 13

How to manufacture your product idea or invention.

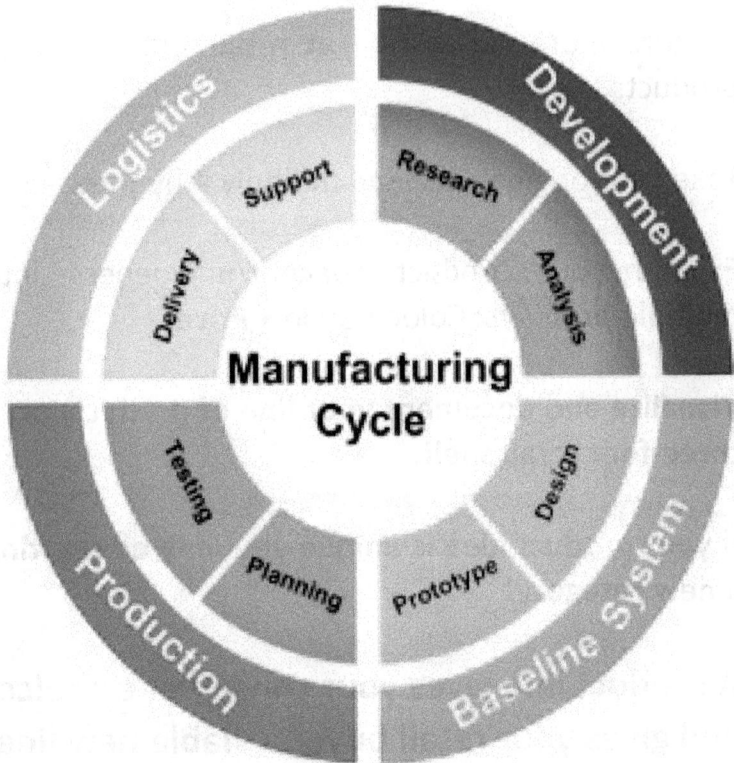

I have been involved in sourcing and manufacturing products both here in the USA and overseas for many years - here is a brief overview:

Your first step, if you decide you want to manufacture your product idea, is to visit a store that carries a similar type of item.

Check out the packaging and find out where the product is made. You may even find the names of manufacturers on the actual packaging.

Check out the quality of the products.

Then do research over the web.

Research **CUSTOM** manufacturers (manufacturers who make products for other companies) and companies who specialize in your type of product.

There are global sourcing web companies who you can simply request manufacturing information on any type of product and you will receive many replies and scores of choices.

Don't make any decisions until you have received quality product samples – and have agreed upon ALL the manufacturing costs.

If your product is made up of multiple parts then you may have to research a different manufacturer for each material.

Plastic molded products require molds and, depending on the size of the mold, this can be an expensive process. The smaller the mold- the less the cost.

Domestic Manufacturers

The advantage of manufacturing domestically is the cost savings in freight. Which can be quite substantial if your product is large.

Domestic manufacturing also provides a much quicker shipping window. So you can get your product into the retailers' warehouses quickly and efficiently.

There is also the advantage of being able to keep a close watch on the manufacturing process.

Overseas Manufacturers

The advantage of manufacturing your product overseas is the **cost savings involved** in the actual manufacturing of the item.

However, your shipping timeframe is considerably longer – **90 days:**

30 days to order the materials
30 days to manufacture the product
30 days to ship the product to a coastal USA port.

Then you have to ship the product from the coastal warehouse to your USA warehouse/s.

You will also have the extra travel costs involved in working with overseas factories during the design and manufacturing stages.
However, first you can get the factories to **send you product samples for approval before you make any commitment.**
Once your have received product samples – you can get accurate per unit costs.

The Canton Fair (Chinese Export Commodities Fair – www.cantonfair.org) is an ideal Show to attend in Guangzhou, China.
There are 100,000 kinds of Chinese goods exhibited there. You will need an invitation and a visa to attend. (See Chapter 23)

The manufacturer you choose to manufacture your product may not offer Warehouse, Shipping and Distribution services. But you can contract with other companies who will handle this for you.

CHAPTER 14

TIPS ON HOW TO LICENSE YOUR PRODUCT IDEA

WHEN YOU COME UP WITH A VIABLE PRODUCT IDEA YOU MAY HAVE A CHOICE:

• Licensing your product

• Manufacturing, marketing and selling your product yourself

In the past I have successfully licensed a number of product ideas into various products categories – clocks, games, calendars & toys.

Here is what I learned along the way.

The advantages of licensing your product idea

1. It takes away the pressure of you having to manufacture, market, and distribute the product yourself.

2. Reduces your development costs and gives you a royalty income stream. (5 -10%)

3. Your licensor has an established reputation in the marketplace – so your product idea has instant credibility

4. Your licensor has an established sales force – so your product gets to market more quickly.

5. Your licensor is responsible for marketing and advertising your product – thereby achieving instant consumer awareness for your product.

The disadvantages of licensing your product idea

1.You may lose control of the final product design.

2.You are dependent on the licensor to

manufacturer the product to the quality you may expect.

3.Licensors often have hundreds of new licensed products to introduce every year and yours may get lost in the shuffle.

4.You are dependent on the licensor to market, promote and advertise your product – which is often calculated on a particular product's initial sales projections.

Before you can license your idea – you must have done the following:

1.Developed your product idea to a tangible stage whereby a potential licensor (or licensing agent) can touch and feel the product. I.e. a prototype or sample.

2.Documented all your product, category and industry research and have become an expert in these fields.

3.Developed your product idea into a product line (choices)

4.Developed your product and packaging design.

5. Developed your BRAND – yes licensors will license a new brand if it is well executed – enabling you to continue to add new products to the license- The products I licensed had all been developed through to a Brand image.

5.Executed all your legal documents: patents (if applicable)
Copyrights on all designs and images

6.Researched all possible licensors in your products' category

7.Researched licensing agents who specialize in your products' category – If you have no reputation in the licensing or product development fields you will most probably have to work with an agent. – Make sure you have all agents you meet sign confidentiality agreement.

Setting your Royalty Rates

Industry: What is the industry standard royalty rate? Based on a recent study, the medium royalty rate across all industries is 4.5% from a low 2.8% in the food industry to a high of 8% in the media and entertainment industry.

Importance: Is it a breakthrough or core product — minor or major improvement to competitive products?

Uniqueness: Does it have patents, copyrights etc.

State of Development: How much more R & D or clearance does the product require before it can be used by consumers?

Risk: Will it work?

Profit Margins: Volume vs. specialty.

What must you consider when entering into a licensing agreement?

Do you offer **exclusivity? Or is the license shared?**

Territorial Scope: Do you offer them just the domestic market — or are they worldwide distributors?

Do you insist on an **advance against royalties? Or is the license based entirely on earnings?**

What will be the **term** of the license? – 1 year, 3 year? Etc.

Market Scope: How many fields can the invention be exploited.

Will the license have an automatic renewal after the term expires? Do you want to include a performance clause in order for the license to be renewed?

CHAPTER 15

BEGINNERS GUIDE TO TRADE SHOWS

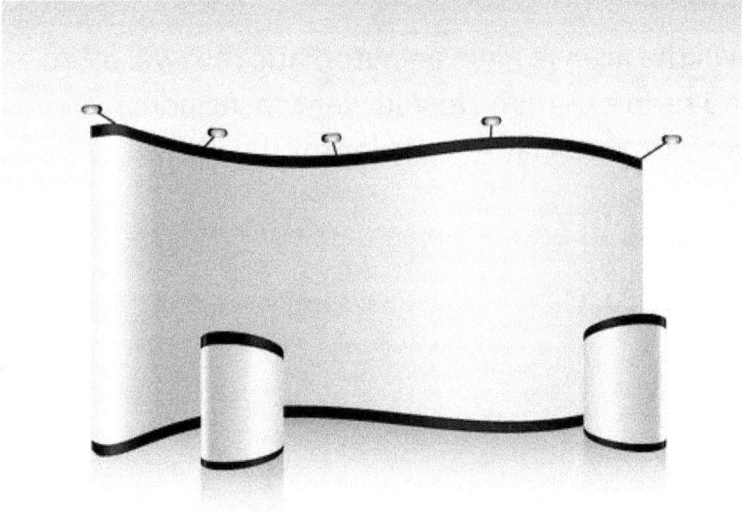

Your exhibit booth is your billboard for your brand and company image.

The more professional it looks – the more credible your product and brand are perceived.

There are two types of trade shows:

Industry Trade Shows – Usually not open to the public. Just buyers and exhibitors are allowed to attend and must be registered prior to attending. I.e. Housewares Show, NACDS, Toy Fair etc.

Consumer Trade Shows – For the general public. E.g. Home Show, Surf and Dive Show etc. An opportunity to exhibit your company, products and brand and create added consumer awareness.

When you have developed your products and have created your brand and company image – it is time to "go to the show".

Industry Trade Shows offer you three major opportunities:

1.   Exposing your products to your buyers
2.   Interviewing and hiring independent reps
3.   Meeting the press – PR opportunities

In order to establish which industry trade show you should attend – do your research.

First you need to know what industry your product is best suited to i.e. sporting goods, cosmetics, clothing etc.

Once you have established the industry – research what are the three major trade shows for this industry.

Your end goal is to register for the show that best suits your needs i.e. it is cost effective and will enable you to expose your product to your potential buyers.

The trade show organizers will send you a show package which provides you with all the necessary information – Booth space sizes, power, set up times, cleaning services labor, show events, press attendees, etc.

You will have to book a booth space – so you will need to decide what style booth and what size space you need.

You have three types of booths to choose from:

(1) A trade show's standard booth (provided) Usually a 10ft x 10ft booth space and features: 6 ft. table draped back wall and sides, carpet, signage – name of your company (No logo)

(2) Rent a booth from an exhibit booth company:

Many choices to choose from a simple Pop up booth – easy to assemble by yourself or a more substantial booth that would require you to hire trade show labor to assemble and disassemble.

(3) Have a custom booth created and built to your specifications. Ideal scenario if you are going to be exhibiting at shows on a regular basis. It also enables you to feature your products and brand to their best advantage.

For your first trade show you may want to keep costs to a minimum – a simple hired "pop up" booth with lights and graphics in a 10x10ft space is all you need.

You will not have to pay for labor and can set it up and break it down yourself. Spend your money on your graphics, presentation, promotional displays, press releases and a carpet for your space if the carpet color is not complimentary to your graphics.

When your product is established in the marketplace then splurge on a custom booth –

CHAPTER 16

SALES TIPS AND SECRETS -YOU WISH YOU KNEW

My Mother sold Encyclopedias door to door when I was a small child. When she left with a "sale" she also left with a new "best friend".

She was still doing telephone sales in her early 80s and loving it. I learned from the best.

I have been in the sales business almost all of my adult life.

My sales career has taken me from door to door "cold calling" in New Zealand to selling multi million dollars of products to the mass-market retailers of the USA, Canada and Europe.

I have worked as an employee, an independent consultant, and president and owner of my own companies. Always "sales" was my strength. My ability to "sell-in" was a major player in the success of many product launches into the world market.

These are my secret sales tips I have learned along the way.

Before making a sales call – be prepared

Research the company and the buyer to whom you will be selling your product. Create a file on this buyer. Qualify the buyer – is he or she the decision maker? If not – who is?

Do your sales check list: Are the following materials current, relevant and complete?
Product Samples • Sales Materials • Promotional Materials Product.

Are all the materials easily accessible? (You don't want to be fumbling around in a briefcase looking for relevant information when asked.)

Are your files in a tidy, professional briefcase or

appropriate folder?

Do your personal check! Is your attire appropriate and professional? Remember YOU are your PRODUCT or SERVICE in the buyer's eyes. First impressions can be lasting impressions – your attire shows your respect for the buyer and the company you represent.

Your appointment: Always be early for your appointment. You can learn more about your buyer and his company by observing staff from the waiting room. It also allows you time to begin a relationship with the front desk personnel (who often set up the appointments with your buyer). If you are cold calling on the account/buyer - introduce yourself and your company and establish if this is a good time to visit or if a more appropriate time is suitable – respect your buyer's time before your own.

Meeting the buyer. Look the buyer straight in the eyes and introduce yourself and your company and the purpose of your visit – keep it short and to the point. You should have practiced your "one sentence" that describes your product" prior to making sales calls.

Do not "crowd" the buyer. Respect your buyer's

space. No one likes a salesperson in his or her face. Move your chair back if it is too close to the buyer and place your briefcase in front of you. Do not enter the buyer's personal space by passing him or her your products or sales materials until your have established a mutual alliance.

Tell your story first. Stories sell – facts tell. Your sales pitch should be a "short story" with a beginning a middle and an end. Your story should cover: Who you and your company are/ what is your product and its history, who is your product's consumer, (Ensure your product's consumer is also your buyer's consumer.)

Establish credibility. You are your product's expert. You are the expert in your product's industry. Share your research and product knowledge to establish credibility with your buyer.

Establish a relationship. Your buyer/account research has given you information that can establish mutual ground. What is the buyer's main focus as it pertains to your product's industry? This focus should be your focus during the meeting.

Ask questions. The more you can learn about what your buyer's needs are, the more you can meet them. Take notes if the buyer is giving you important information. It shows that you take his information seriously.

Be prepared to react. If the buyer is giving you information that indicates your product/company does not meet his needs — ask why? Take notes. Once you know the problem you can solve it. You learn more from the negatives than you do the positives.

Ask multi-choice questions. When presenting your product give a choice when asking a question — i.e. "Which color do your prefer, black or white?" This prevents a negative answer.

Don't ask a single question until you know you will get a positive answer. Once you get a "NO" your buyer has made a negative decision. **"NO's" tend to build upon themselves.** Don't build this blockade.

Don't waste your buyer's time. Keep your presentation — short, professional, informative and to the point. You want to establish a repeat relationship with the buyer.

Become your buyer's source of information. At every sales call establish yourself as the professional in your field. Always ensure that you have provided the buyer with fresh, relevant information that your buyer can share with his upper management.

Read your buyer.
- Creative – Product orientated
- Analytical – Information/results driven
- New to the position – little experience
- Experienced – Expert in his field

Begin with the lowest price point. (I know you think it is better going high first. but it isn't) Establish a "higher perceived value" from the onset. Prove added value with each price increase.

Do a quick overview first. Begin the actual product presentation with a quick overview of what the products are, the product range, product attributes and product features. This establishes a meeting agenda and allows the buyer to focus in on what products he is the most interested in.

Establish buyer interest. Read body language. Do not proceed with a more detailed product presentation without buyer interest. Return to industry statistics and build a more solid case for your product's viability.

Buyer/account needs. Ask what your buyer's

needs are i.e. take notes.
- Advertising/promotional requirements
- Merchandising/in store display opportunities
- Sell through percentages
- Seasonal vs. Everyday opportunities

Prove your product's viability. **Provide documented focus group** information. Show visuals of consumers using your product/service and their comments.

Product costs are no secret. Today buyers have access to manufacturing costs – from both domestic and overseas manufacturers. Keep your product costs real. Buyers accept that branded products have added value and added costs.

Keep prices honest. One price for each distribution channel.
- Mass market retailers
- Specialty stores
- Distributors
- International distributors
- Online retailers

Lose credibility – your lose the account!

Ask the right questions. You have researched his account and know what questions to ask that relate to your product, your product's industry and what this account may require of you.

I.e. freight, turns, warehousing, new store allowances, co-op advertising allowances etc. Ask these questions now so you are prepared when it comes time to ship the product.

Confirm all positive responses. Repeat back to the buyer all the positive responses he/she made during the meeting i.e.

- Your Company is focusing on teen consumers.
- You are increasing your shelf space to accommodate more teen products.
- You are focusing on $9.99 - $19.9 retail price points
- You are also focusing on branded products
- You see our category as an everyday item
- You will be doing major promotions in this category

Match positive responses to your product i.e.
- 95% of teens focused say they would purchase our products
- Our product falls into your preferred price points
- 93% of teens own at least one of our products
- 92% of teens use our product everyday
- Back to school and Christmas are tens most popular promotional periods.

Ask for the order! (You would be surprised how many salespeople don't ask for the order.) There are many ways to do this.

• So you would be interested in the $9.99 and $14.99 price points?

• You see these as everyday items?

•Would you also like to promote these at the Back to School promotional periods.

• When would you require the products to be in your stores?

Take detailed notes as the buyer is providing this information.

Leave as soon as you have a buying commitment! Don't dilly dally – you can confirm all the follow up information in an email following the meeting. Overstaying your welcome is NOT an option. Shake the buyer's hand and thank him/her for their time and let them know that you will follow up with all the details discussed at the meeting. You don't want to give the buyer extra work. Make buying from you easy, effective and profitable.

Sales call follow up! As soon as you leave the meting – type out a call report. This report covers ALL discussion during the meeting and all the meeting points. Also a full description of the buyer and the account. This report is for you (and your boss's eyes) only.

Buyer follow up!   Send a follow up email to the buyer.   This report covers all AGREED UPON discussion points of the meeting.   Remember that you want to make it easy and efficient for the buyer to do business with you.   Don't ask the buyer to do any extra work on your behalf. Let the buyer know that you are there to assist in any way he needs.

CHAPTER 17

TRAITS OF A SUCCESSFUL SALESPERSON

Always Prepared. Always arrives early for the meeting with current sales materials, buyer/account background and extra samples and materials for attendees.

Pre-arranged meeting room scheduled. Getting a buyer out of his office into a mutual meeting area creates a more effective buying atmosphere. Allows for additional set-up time.

Knows that **SELL-IN** does not mean **SELL-THROUGH**

Does not CROWD the buyer during the presentation

ONLY asks the buyer a QUESTION when he/she knows the answer will be a positive one

Tells a story in the presentation – Facts Tell – Stories Sell

Always asks for the Sale

Provide an internal follow-up with a detailed call report after EVERY sales call.

Immediate follow up with buyer (or rep) confirming ALL points discussed and agreed upon during the meeting.

Always respects the buyer and the sales representative – they are the experts in their field

CHAPTER 18
HIRING YOUR NATIONAL SALES FORCE

Hiring your Independent Sales Representatives is one of the MOST IMPORTANT stages of getting your IDEA to MARKET

My expertise has always been in selling large volume of products to the mass market and the most cost effective way to set up a sales force is to use Independent Rep Agencies. Their relationship with your major Retail Buyers is critical to your product's future success.

Many of the mass market independent rep companies already represent up to sixty lines that they are currently selling to the retail customers in their territory and may not want to add new lines to their current work load. They may also be selling a competitive line to yours, which would prevent you from using them.

Also many of these rep companies will not be prepared to take on an unknown line from an unknown manufacturer. It is not an easy task. However, if you persevere and can convince them of your product's potential success, you may be in luck.

Independent Rep companies cover from one to ten states depending on their territory. Each rep company has anywhere from one to fifteen sales reps working within their company

• Check out your industry's MANUFACTURERS Association for Independent Sales Representatives who specialize in your type of product.

• Check out your product's industry for TRADE MAGAZINES and TRADE SHOWS for Independent Sales Representative contacts

• Have ALL potential Independent Sales Representatives SIGN a CONFIDENTIALITY Agreement

• Ensure ALL your Independent Sales Representatives SIGN an INDEPENDENT REPRESENTATIVE AGREEMENT upon hiring.

• Why an Independent Sales Representative rather than an in-house sales person? An Independent Sales Representative works off a percentage of sales – he pays his own expenses. YOU have to pay for all expenses and commissions for an in-house salesperson.

• Confirm your Independent Sales Representative DOES NOT represent a COMPETITIVE product line.

• Confirm your Independent Sales Representative lives in the SAME CITY as your BUYERS' corporate offices.

• Always RESPECT your salesperson and your buyer. Know that although you are paying commissions to your Independent Sales Representative – he is always working with his buyer's best interest in mind – The buyer ultimately controls his income.

• Independent Sales Representatives have the EXPERIENCE and CONTACTS you need to sell in your products to the buyers in their territory.

• Independent Sales Representatives are a necessary BUFFER between you and your buyer.

CHAPTER 19

CREATIVE FRUSTRATION – HITTING THE WALL!

It happens!
You are in the middle of a creative and productive frenzy and suddenly – you hit the wall!

Your adrenalin has been pumping for days, even weeks. You have been on a new creative adventure and then suddenly the bubble bursts...

Clarity sets in.   Your enthusiasm is replaced with

horror.

"Why didn't I see this coming?" You scold yourself. "This is just too hard. I need to bring in an expert."

Then you remind yourself just who you are: An explorer of ideas, an adventurer on the seas of inspiration, a warrior in the battle of creative obstacles.

And you have learned – a wall is there for a reason. Its purpose is to create a new path of opportunity. It is just a way of your intuitive mind telling you to "Stop! Clear your mind! Take a rest! Let your creativity free! Let it breathe again!

An idea is born in an instant. We nurture it with constant attention.

However, there is a fine line between nurturing and smothering.

"To express yourself in a creative way you don't need structure you need an empty mind." Quote by E'yen A Gardner.

As we develop our idea into a viable entity... our

minds expand to accommodate the vast amounts of necessary research and information.

All this new information can become tangled causing our progress to be stunted.

As the great Albert Einstein said. "The Mind that opens to a new idea never returns to its original size.

So stop, breathe and clear your mind when you hit the wall.

It is our mind's gentle reminder that although we have 70,000 thoughts a day and 1.5 thoughts a minute – we need to be thinking them with clarity.

And don't you find – when your mind has become clear again... the obstacle is removed – just like magic?

CHAPTER 20
10 TIPS FOR GIVING A SPEECH

Being in sales and marketing often requires giving a speech or two.

When you have to give a speech – It is often more successful when you have prepared just a general topic synopsis and then, if you can, free flow.

(1) "The best way to sound like you know what you're talking about is to know what you're talking about." ~Author Unknown

Oh how true. I find that whenever I have to give a

talk – It is more successful when I have prepared just a general topic synopsis and then completely free flow... If you know your subject really well, it takes a natural course and the audience enjoys the ride with you.

(2)" Always be shorter than anybody dared to hope". ~Lord Reading, on speechmaking

"Make sure you have finished speaking before your audience has finished listening." Dorothy Sarnoff

Keep an eye on your audience. If they are not spellbound and have direct eye contact –then you have overstayed your welcome.

(3) "Speech is the mirror of the soul; as a man speaks, so is he." Publilius Syrus

What the heart thinks, the tongue speaks" Romanian Proverb

Show your personality. Let the audience know "who you are" as well as "what you are".

Personalize your points with stories of experience and humor.

(4) "The eloquent man is he who is no beautiful speaker, but who is inwardly and desperately drunk with a certain belief". ~Ralph Waldo Emerson

If you have passion and an honest belief in your subject – it will show through. Share that passion.

(5) "Share your knowledge. It is a way to achieve immortality." Dalai Lama X1V—

I love this quote!! One of my favorites. We are in a kinder place in the world now. Sharing our wisdom, our experiences and our knowledge is like throwing seed into a fresh, fertile meadow.

(6) Facts Tell and Stories Tell

Tell your story, share your journey. **Your audience will remember your story more than they do statistics and figures. Your story adds a human element to your speech.**

(7)"It takes a lot of courage to show your dreams to someone else. " Erma Bombeck

"Vulnerability is the birthplace of innovation, creativity and change." – Brene Brown

Oh how true.

Do not fear to show your vulnerability. It is what makes us human and allows us to relate to our audience.

(8) Where to focus your attention when speechmaking.

I know that when you are selling to a group of potential buyers. You do not sell the ones that are smiling and nodding at you – but rather you concentrate on the ones that have yet to be convinced.

I find the opposite when I am giving a speech. I am transfixed to the smiling faces. They give me the courage and the support I need and energize my confidence.

(9) Have fun.

When the audience sees you having a wonderful time...they have a wonderful time.

(10) Be the expert in your field.   Research your

topic well before your presentation.

To be credible is to be confident in your knowledge.

CHAPTER 21

TRAITS OF AN INSPIRATIONAL THINKER

The uncompromising need to surround yourself with POSITIVE people

The avoidance of NEGATIVITY at all costs.

The ability to see the BEST in all situations

Owning a super powered strength of RECOVERY in the face of adversity

Believing that TODAY is going to be the BEST DAY of

your life

Being able to live in the moment knowing that you have already set your FUTURE in motion

Keeping the window of your mind open to allow future knowledge and past experiences to co-mingle and create delectable MOMENTS of PURE CLARITY

Knowing an IDEA is created in less than a second and once captured in the mind's eye – can be the BASIS of something wonderful.

Being able to absorb vast amounts of information and condense it down to a simple UNDERSTANDING of a subject

The need to have a PROJECT to CREATE and COMPLETE at all times

CHAPTER 22
DON'T MURKY UP YOUR BRAND

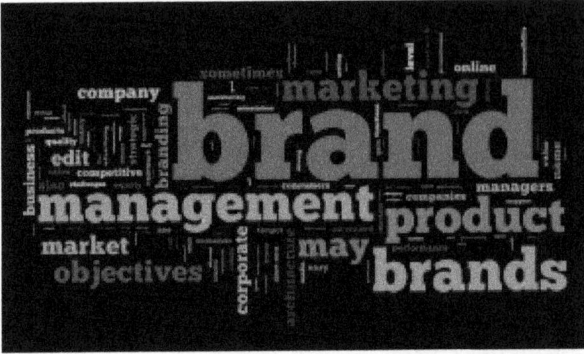

It happens.   Life is complicated.   Your vision gets confused and your brand becomes murky.

It is so easy to do – your enthusiasm takes over and, before your know it, you have added so many products or services that your brand has begun to lose its identity.

Maybe you want to freshen up your brand so you set out to shop for those special ingredients written in black and white in your trusted recipe book.   You have made the recipe before and it works. It is sheer perfection.

The problem is, once you get to the marketplace you are tempted by all the new ingredients that are offered. Ingredients that are not in your recipe but are so exciting and different that you start picking and choosing them at random.

Your brand basket becomes full to overflowing with ingredients that hold so much promise. Their colors and aromas are full of potential. You can't wait to get home to start adding them to your recipe.

You place your recipe on the counter and begin to remove the shiny new ingredients from your shopping basket. You look down at the assortment of ingredients in front of you and realize that you have three options; combine the ingredients into one, create a whole new recipe or keep to your original recipe.

A brand is constant, a brand earns trust and familiarity, and a brand has a clear message – a message your consumers understand.

If you want to add new and fresh ingredients make sure that you have **tested them first.**

Do they improve/freshen the original recipe? Can your customers still recognize the recipe? Maybe you can add the new ingredients as a side dish. Make sure that your choices have been tasted and approved.

Random decisions result in a murky brand.

CHAPTER 23

CHINA SOURCING FAIRS

THE CANTON FAIR
CHINA IMPORT AND EXPORT FAIR

(Canton Fair Complex for short), the largest modernized exhibition center in Asia, is located in Pazhou Island, Guangzhou, China. It is a perfect integration of human and ecological concerns and high technology, sparkling the world like a shining star.

The complex covers a total construction area of 1,100,000 M^2 with the indoor exhibition area of 338,000 M^2 and the outdoor exhibition area of 43,600 M^2. The Area A has an indoor exhibition area of 130,000 M^2 and an outdoor exhibition area of 30,000 M^2, the Area B has an indoor exhibition area of 128,000 M^2 and an outdoor exhibition area of 13,600 M^2, and the Area C has an indoor exhibition area of 80,000 M^2.

Address: No. 380, Yuejiang Zhong Road, Guangzhou, China

Chinese exhibitors of the Canton Fair boast good credibility and strength. Over 24,000 Chinese enterprises attend each session of the Fair.

Among them, manufacturers account for 51%; foreign trade enterprises account for 38%; industrial trade enterprises account for 10%

Has an exhibition area of 1.18 million square meters, the 116th session of the Canton Fair had over 60,000 exhibition stands, attracting 24,840 exhibitors from both home and abroad?

China Import and Export Fair, also known as the Canton Fair, is held biannually in Guangzhou every spring and autumn, with a history of 55 years since 1957.

The Fair is a comprehensive one with the longest history, the highest level, the largest scale, the most complete exhibit variety, the broadest distribution of overseas buyers and the greatest business turnover in China.

You need an invitation and a visa to attend which is easily arranged through their website

For more information: http://www.cantonfair.org.cn

global✺sources

Global Sources Summit

For online & Amazon sellers
Co-located with trade shows

79,000+ buyers from 153 countries and territories visited 8,500 booths at previous trade shows in Hong Kong. You can source the latest products, and start selling them on Amazon.

For information on the Global Sourcing Fair see website: http://www.globalsources.com

Remember that the lead-time to get your products to your retailers is longer than manufacturing your products domestically.

Lead times expected:

30 days to source your product
30 days to manufacture your product
30 days to ship your product to a USA port.

CHAPTER 24

YOUR PRODUCT NEEDS AN INDUSTRY

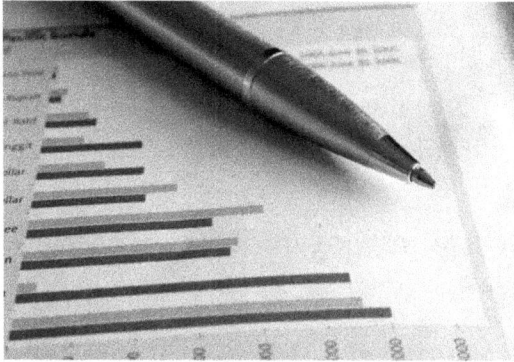

The product and the industry go hand in hand.

It is imperative that you **know your industry** if you are going to be successful selling your product in the marketplace.

So you have a product idea or invention and want to know where to start? You start first by visualizing the idea in its final resting place. If you don't know where that is then now is a good time to find out.

What industry you will be selling your item to?

Start doing Google searches within that industry.

Start researching, documenting, printing and filing the information for future reference.

The size of the industry.

You need this information so that you can find out the potential sales volume you could achieve within this industry.

Is the industry growing or declining? – by what percentage?

If the industry is in a growth spurt – buyers will be looking to add new products

If the industry is in a decline – this can also be an opportunity if your product is innovative enough to stimulate sales and breathe life into a tired industry.

What are the best selling items within this industry?

This enables you to study consumer reaction to the category – what is selling is what your consumer wants.

Why are these items outselling others within the category?

What are your marketing opportunities within the industry?

Check out all the trade magazines and websites.

Make sure that you are using social media within your specific industry.

What trade shows or events promote the products within the industry?

Research all relevant trade shows (both buyer and consumer shows) for your particular industry.

Check availability, costs, booth rentals, space rentals, dates.

Document all your statistics
Keep all this information filed away in a 3 ring binder for quick reference. Highlight the major points. This information is critical for your sales materials, financials, sales projections, manufacturing projections etc.

Become an expert in your industry
Your buyers will expect you to know your industry.

ABOUT THE AUTHOR

Leonie Mateer

Puppeteer, children's entertainer, owner of a model agency, TV talk show panelist, luxury accommodation owner, entrepreneur: storyteller Leonie Mateer has lived a full and diverse life. Born and raised in New Zealand, Mateer moved to the United States in her 30s to pursue business opportunities. She returned to New Zealand for several years in the 2000s, owning and operating a luxury lodge in Northland - which has been an inspiration for her crime series - and now splits her time between Northland and the United States.

Mateer is known for her huge success as a brand development expert, and has previously written business advice books.

Leonie Mateer is the creator of the brand, Caboodles™ - a teen girl brand that took the retail industry by storm in the late 1980s and early 90s.

She was named in the 'Who's Who' of both Leading American Executives and American Inventors in the 1990s.

"HAVE A PRODUCT IDEA? - HOW MANY COULD YOU SELL? Is a collection of business blogs she has written and which have generated hundreds of thousands of readers over the past many years. Each chapter is a product development and marketing gem - from tips for protecting your product idea to getting your product on the shelves of Wal-Mart, Target, K-Mart and more... A must read for first time inventors!

A lifelong storyteller, she published "The Murder Suite", her first adult thriller, in 2013, kick starting a five- book series starring Audrey, "a psychopath, a serial killer and a friendly resident in a small town in rural Northland".

Other books include:
• Psoriasis – The Simple Cure – Who Knew? – Health/Diet
• The Caboodles Blueprint - How to turn your idea into millions - Business
• The Magical World of Dantonia - A mid-grade fantasy novel
• Black Lake – A mid-grade thriller
• Read Your Own Fortune & Read Your Own Financial Fortune – New Age

Ms. Mateer lives in Ventura, California and Northland, New Zealand.

If you found the information in this book helpful, I would love you to leave a review on Amazon. Thanking You.

100 Top Retailers
All retail store numbers based on Kantar Retail Research and Company reports. Source Kantar Retail.